The Very Stuff

Stephen Beal

The Very Stuff

Poems on color, thread, and the habits of women

INTERWEAVE PRESS

Cover and interior design by Signorella Graphic Arts.
Cover photo by Joe Coca, ©1995 by Joe Coca & IWP, Inc.
Production by Marc McCoy Owens.

 Interweave Press
201 East Fourth Street
Loveland, Colorado 80537
USA

Printed in Hong Kong

Library of Congress Cataloging-in-Publication Data:

Beal, Stephen, 1939–
     The very stuff : poems on color, thread, and the habits of women /
Stephen Beal.
        p.   cm.
     ISBN 1-883010-16-0
     1. Embroidery—Poetry.   2. Women—Poetry.   I. Title.
PS3552.E136V4   1995
811'.43–dc20   95-21891
                                                                          CIP

First Printing: 10M: 995:CC

The titles of the poems in this collection are numbers that identify shades of cotton embroidery floss manufactured by Dollfus, Mieg Company (DMC), Paris, France, whose kind support of this endeavor is gratefully acknowledged.

for Linda Ligon

"I remember a house where all were good to me. . . ."
—*Gerard Manley Hopkins*

Preface

I was born in Illinois but I came to consciousness in Pittsburgh, where my family lived during World War II. My father could not serve in the armed forces because he was diabetic, so, to do his part, he was working for a steel company.

Our first home in Pittsburgh was an apartment on the second floor of a Victorian house on the corner of Linden and Edgerton Avenues. This corner holds my first memory in the world: coming home with Mother from a bus ride downtown. A light rain is falling and I have run across Linden ahead of her. When I look back, she is standing on the corner, holding up her purse to protect her hat from the rain. Her hat is made of water lilies, big white petals, shaggy yellow centers.

I want to hold that hat. As a child I want to hold it. As a man I want to hold it. I want that stuff in my hands. From my earliest days I have delighted in the color and the texture of dyed fiber. Dyed fiber has been my delight since the days I had *no* memory. I have been told that when I was two, my favorite plaything at Grandmother Beal's house was spools of silk thread from her sewing cabinet. I have been told that I said my first word while pulling pink toilet paper onto the floor of a bathroom in her house. "Pretty," I said, surrounded by streamers of pink.

Now I'm not maintaining that I was fated to write poems about colors of fiber, but I will say it fits. It feels good. I just love this stuff. Remember Donald Duck's uncle, Scrooge McDuck? Uncle Scrooge was a millionaire, and a miser, and his favorite pastime was going down to his vault where he threw his money into the air and let it bounce off his head, or burrowed through his money like a gopher. That's how I feel about colored thread and colored fabric. I want to wrap myself up in it. I want to get inside it. I want to hold it and use it and make beautiful things of it. I want to celebrate it. I want to say this stuff is joy.

There are forty-three poems here, and they are first of all celebrations of color, celebrations of the very stuff I hold in my hands when I embroider.

The poems are also celebrations of life, the good things of this world with which I associate colors. The poems incorporate movie references because, in the early 1940s, movies were the place that color overwhelmed me. Big hunks and swatches of color zooming out from the screen. The poems incorporate clothes that women wore. Women's clothes were another primary source for color. They were also a place that I could hold color, stroke color, pick color up and look through color. Then my parents gave me crayons, and I was gone.

Unfortunately, I was a good student and a boy, and good boy students in the 1940s and 1950s, good boy students who were expected to attend a Respectable College and Make Something Of Their Lives—well, it just wasn't fitting that such boys care about color. I mean, caring about color was *okay*, it was nice to have another interest, but surely you couldn't base your life on color. You couldn't be a painter or a dyer or a fabric designer or a couturier. Could you? Not to the people by and among whom I was raised. Not to the boy I was then. To all of us, boys like me supported themselves by going to work, by getting good jobs, by doing chores at desks with paper.

So I became a writer, which was the closest I could come to doing something at a desk that interested me. But deep at the fiber of my being, like the pink toilet paper and the spools of silk thread before I came to consciousness, like Mother's water-lily hat and some pieces of chiffon in a box in her bottom drawer when I was a toddler, like all the subsequent colors I saw on people, usually on women because it is still women who wear color *for* color, deep where I wanted to be, where I felt most comfortable with and as myself, in that place there was . . .

. . . there was 972, the first color I wrote a poem for. I was stitching a Mediterranean room, and for a stairwell opening off the back of this room I employed 972. I'd never used the color before. This thick rich golden yellow took over the picture, throbbed and glowed like a jolly spacecraft coming in to take a look around. The color was so powerful and so magic and so good that I had to write a poem for it.

I read "972" at a fiber lecture that summer, and it was well received. In November I thought to myself, Hey, your favorite red is 817. You've done three canvases based on 817. Doesn't 817 deserve a poem?

Then DMC asked me to submit slides of canvases for an international fiber exhibition they were sponsoring in Japan. I mentioned that I had written a couple of poems about their colors and they said, Send them along. At work a few days later I thought that sending only two poems was mingy. So I went to a computer and wrote two more. 924. 747. That meant I had a yellow, a red, a green, and a blue—and then, within four months, I had twenty-four poems in all.

That was in 1993 and I thought I was done. A couple of the poems were published in *The Flying Needle* and I started reading them at lectures and workshops. Then, late in 1994, PIECEWORK asked to publish five of the poems, and I started writing again. Something there is about approval that starts my creative juices flowing. Say yes to me and I say bounty back.

I would like to acknowledge the many good friends who have encouraged this bounty. Ann Hottelet, Jeane Hutchins, and Julianna Mahley at the Council of American Embroiderers; Ann Caswell at the American Needlepoint Guild; Marie-Pierre Nakamura of Marie-Pierre Designs; Christiane Guglielmazzi at

DMC; Veronica Patterson, editor of PIECEWORK; the folks at Paul Baker Typography; my fellow fiber artists Renie Breskin Adams and Barbara Lee Smith; my readers Vito DePinto, Ann Fay, David Sohn, and Haydée von Sternberg; and my early supporters Elizabeth Vincent Foster, Richard Grunsten, and Joan Comfort Johnson—all have my heartfelt thanks.

Table of Contents

Introduction

A Visit to DMC

At Charles de Gaulle Airport, the pale blue seats in the bus that takes us from the plane to the terminal are 828. On the way to my hotel, the pillars and the girders in the Gare de Lyon Metro stop are 972. Well, 972 shading toward 742. Somewhere between those two strong yellows.

For those who stitch with DMC floss, these will not seem antic observations. Last winter a friend wrote that her new car is 341. At a recent conference, I heard one stitcher tell another, "Just 321 it." For lots of us, the colors of DMC floss represent a means of expressing ourselves not only in embroidery but in thought and speech, and for this reason, for me, a visit to the DMC factory in Mulhouse in Alsace is a visit to old friends. Very old friends. In a drawer in the company archives I see a color card dating back over one hundred years, and the colors on that card are colors we use now. (DMC itself was founded in 1746, by Jean-Henri Dollfuss, the D of DMC; his son Daniel married Anne-Marie Mieg, the M; C stands for Compagnie.) Once DMC manufactures a color, it is never retired. Every color keeps the number originally assigned it. You can count on it: with these threads, your friends are friends for life.

Remember when your college roommate took you home for a visit? When you saw the family, the house, the town your room-mate grew up with? When you started to see dimensions to this person you had only heard about before, or perhaps had never considered? After all, roommates are for now, not then; for here, not there. That's how I feel in Mulhouse. I keep looking for the little pals I work with at home, and what I find in the factory is a carefully-structured process of manufacture. And packaging.

And shipment. I find the business that supports my art, the steady background that enables me to have fun with my pals.

The DMC headquarters resembles a campus, red-brick buildings set amid plane and linden trees, accented with beds of red geranium. A stream runs behind the refectory, built in 1886, and carp jump in the stream. The factory employs 900 people and more green machines than I could ever count.

Everything is done here. Well, almost everything. The cotton is grown in Egypt and the components of the dyes are brought in. But DMC does everything else. The company maintains its own pumping station; the quality of water is a paramount reason for the prominence of Alsatian textile manufacture and DMC recycles waste water for heating the buildings. The cotton arrives constantly from Alexandria, by ship across the Mediterranean to Marseille, then by truck to Mulhouse, so there is always a three-month supply in the warehouse. From bales of cotton to final product (floss, thread, yarn), the process of manufacture and packaging takes about five days; then the products are shipped to distributors and customers throughout the world. (Two-thirds of DMC sales are exports; their biggest floss seller is 666, Christmas red.)

I'm not a businessman and I'm not an engineer, but I can tell you the first thing that impresses me about the factory. It's so clean. Many rows of spinning machines have their very own vacuums, long green automatic tubes that zip up and down the rows sucking up the fluff and lint. I tell you, I am envious of those tubes, desirous. What if I could have a vacuum at home that would never stop, that would just keep sucking up the dust and lint? And the cat hair? And the stuff that walks into the house on shoes? Oh boy.

Well, I can dream about domestic paradises, but what there is before me in Mulhouse is a steady, reliable, faultless process of manufacture that starts with forklifts bringing in 300-pound bales to the mixing machines; they shred the cotton into small tufts and combine them to promote uniformity of color and fiber length. Impurities are removed by a beating machine; then the cotton is carded, combed, drawn, spun, wound, doubled, twisted, and gassed (run through a flame to remove superfluous fibers). These are only eight verbs, but their realization covers many miles of process by green machines, much vigilant super-intendence by DMC personnel.

At the end of the gassing process, the cotton is looped into big loose skeins. Measuring roughly three feet long by a foot wide, the skeins are natural ecru in color, and they are stored in wooden bins that fill a cool shadowed room. When I passed through the Loire Valley on my way back to Paris, I saw herds of white cows slumbering beneath the shade of mighty trees, and the cows reminded me of the skeins of DMC cotton resting in their bins. Along one wall of this vast room, cabinets of little wooden drawers hold samples of stock ecru from the past, each labeled, as are the bins, with the date spun. We opened one drawer: the sample was spun in 1912, and it was fine.

In preparation for dyeing, the skeins are taken from their bins and mercerized, a process introduced to cotton-thread manufacture by a Dollfuss son who learned it in England. Named for the inventor-chemist John Mercer, the process involves bathing the cotton in caustic acid to give it brightness, strength, and affinity for dyeing. After mercerizing, the natural ecru color is bleached out (and dyed back in for floss sold as ecru). During dyeing, the skeins are stretched vertically between bars to ensure color uniformity. Then the dyed skeins head to the dryer, and this is one of my favorite factory scenes. In rows of ten or twelve, the skeins are transported by conveyer belt across a room and up into the air where they wait, row after row of color, like people entering a sports event. Better, like lines of costumed dancers about to go on. The day I'm there, I see 340 or 341, a pale violet, along with some greens, hanging in the air, waiting to enter the dryer. The colors are spring colors, and it is spring outside, and suddenly the whole factory is alive.

Following drying, the cotton is inspected for both penetration and color. A large wooden cabinet adjacent to the drying room holds quality-control samples of each DMC shade—the queen bee of each shade—that the inspector employs for checking color. Once approved, the cotton is wound on cones according to its intended use (floss for embroidery, thread for sewing, balls for crochet and knitting). Being an embroiderer, I follow the floss, and let me tell you, this final process goes very fast. First there are cones of floss, then there are complex machines invented by DMC engineers that, in rapid-fire succession, cut the floss and wind it up into little skeins and slap the labels on either end of each skein and put the skeins in boxes of twenty-four and slap the box labels on and seal them. Then the boxes are packed in cartons and conveyed to logistics for storage or shipment. All told, the factory can produce one million skeins of cotton floss a day.

I tour the manufacturing process in something like three hours of a Wednesday morning, and then I encounter my dearest sight. Down in the basement I see hanks of dyed floss in storage. Once again, like the hanks of stock ecru upstairs, the dyed hanks repose in big wooden bins, row after row of wooden bins, each holding hanks of color in transparent plastic bags. Most bins run counter to the main aisle, but those that run parallel are protected from traffic by linen curtains woven in stripes of ecru and medium blue. Pull back a curtain and there, oh gosh, can you believe it?, there is 3607 beside 817. What a combination, like Marilyn Horne and Placido Domingo.

Such stars. Such colors. Such fun. Thank you, DMC. Thank you for a great performance all around.

The Place Where The Colors Are Made

Someday I will see the place where the colors are made,
    the place of my joy.
There will be stairs leading up, wide marble stairs,
and there will be a room,
vast and vaulted and inspiring,
and there will be music, one hundred strings under the baton
    of Carmen Dragon,
and there will be dancers, one hundred blondes
    gowned by Jean Louis,
whooshing between pillars in pastel chiffon.

This place is it: huge bubbling cauldrons of color
in which innocent cotton is transformed to gaudy hues,
to scarlet and fuchsia, to purple and gold,
to greens that bite your eyes and blues that lead you on until you think
    the world will never end.

Oh, this is it, the place where all your dreams come true,
where nothing is as it was and everything develops the potential
of what it can be.

Here is the stuff of change, the very stuff,
and you can take it home and hold it in your hands.
No paint will do, no paint will ever come close,
when you can stitch your lover a heart of ruby red, and say,
"This is the color—and the texture—of my love for you."

Yes. This is the place where the colors are made.
This is the place of joy.

Oh boy, here's Teddy back again.
Here's a brown so rich and warm and soothing
that you can rest assured in its plush arms.

Here is June earth after rain,
the air ballooning out with the warmth of the sun coming on,
with the scent of peony and iris from the garden,
with the scent of syringa from the hedge,
with the scent of corn from the fields beyond,
the corn coming on strong and sturdy from the rich brown earth,
this earth, the source that feeds and holds us all.

Oh, let there be nothing on earth but earth,
brown earth, this earth,
swelling out from Iowa and Illinois,
watered by the Mississippi Basin,
cherished at the heart of the country,
held at the very being of the country—
as a child holds a beloved bear.

All good reds should be dresses, and there's an end to that.
If it shouldn't be a dress, it isn't red.
It's maroon, or purple, or brown.
It's something you would see on a man, around his neck,
whereas the places that you see good reds are
	all around a woman,
and if that sounds sexist, too bad—
too bad for all the breasts and butts and bellies in this world
done up in red to be undone, to be enjoyed,
too bad for all the juice and joy of love,
once you get through the red.

But what about the butts and bellies of men?
Don't they look good in red?

Of course they do—
but, so far, the only way you'll see a man in red the way that
	you see women in red
is in opera, or No, or some fantastic futuristic film
where the hero takes your breath away—
not because he's powerful, or good, or smart, or clever,
but because he's wearing red, red all over,
and he is looking like a god.

I tell you, the liberation I am after is
	the liberation of red.
Yes!
I am all for everybody wearing red whenever they can,
as much as they can,

men striding down our streets in red kimonos embroidered with
    gold dragons,
hooking up with women wearing red kimonos embroidered with
    gold dragons,
or hooking up with men wearing red kimonos embroidered with
    gold dragons,
while women wearing red kimonos embroidered with gold dragons
are hooking up with women wearing red kimonos embroidered with
    gold dragons,
and all these immortal couples are striding on to Olympus,
to Valhalla,
to the Heaven everyone aspires to,
and everyone will reach,
on the good red wings of immortal love.

309

It doesn't look like tulle, and it doesn't scratch,
my little skein of 309,
but this sweet, tender red is the shade of Mary Ann's formal
    the first time we went to a dance, in high school,
on the waxed brown battleship linoleum of Social Hall.
Mary Ann had had an operation on her eye—the white
of her eye was blue, and disturbing—
so I held her tight for the slow dances, and got scratched,
and when we bopped I watched the way her black hair fell
    across her cheek,
but I did not look at her eye.

Why was this beauty so assaulted?—
reeling from our love that did not work to the love of other
    men whose love did not work,
moving on from Evanston and Wellesley to Berkeley,
where nothing worked, not in the sixties—not working
    was the Berkeley point—
and fetching up in England, where she married, and gave birth
    to a girl and a boy,
and died, all in the space of six or seven years, the cancer
    metastasizing from her breasts to her liver, dead in pain,
a beautiful young mother of thirty-six.

Whose smile is radiant. I can see it from here, in her photo on
    the bookshelf,
and tonight I'm having dinner with her daughter.

Rebecca is a student in Chicago now, where, her stepmother
     says, there's been a spot of trouble with a man.
Rebecca's chestnut hair is brushed with red, but it grows on her
     temples the way that Mary Ann's did.
     It is thick like Mary Ann's hair,
     and there can be the same flash of glee in Rebecca's blue eyes.
Pure glee. As though you have said what she's been waiting
     all her life to hear.
As though now she knows.

Now she knows. You don't get on without pain.
There are prices for joy.
We used to go for snacks after highbrow movies, Mary Ann and I,
and we would sit in booths in coffee shops on Chicago's
     near north side,
and she would ask me questions,
and I would say, I don't know.

But I do. Rebecca, too.
It's okay, Mary Ann. All of us are working it through.

This is the color of my good cat Gus,
who died last fall, age nineteen and a half.
Gus was a swell companion, an easygoing fellow,
nothing like our stressed-out buddy Peter, who died ten years ago.

I would be stitching, and Peter, a black tabby,
would be sitting on the table looking out the window—
completely absorbed in his task, completely innocent,
		completely dear—
and the next thing I knew I was fighting for my thread.
The sniper had gotten it
He'd shot me down.
I was on my way out. Rather, Peter's birds were,
		this mighty hunter over the years capturing the thread equivalent
		of goldfinch, bluebird, scarlet tanager, rare green quetzal,
a triumphant rainbow of wet prey hanging off the jaguar's fearsome jaws,
and a wild light in his topaz eyes
as Peter sought to devour the helpless creatures that I rescued
		from his maw,
strand by sopping strand,
lest the tenacious little devil choke to death.

Not Gus. Gus was too mellow for such fuss.
He never bit my thread and he rarely tried to chase it and
		he never chewed on canvases.
He lay in his shoebox on the sofa and scrinched his eyes at me while
		I was stitching in my easy chair. Then he went to sleep.
When it was time for me to move to the sofa to watch
		a movie on the VCR, Gus woke up and invited
		me to scratch his belly.

Then he went back to sleep while I got busy getting entertained,
and when I punched the pause to make some popcorn, Gus also
paused
        to have some crunchies,
and following that snack, and some water, he hopped back in
        his shoebox and went to sleep
while I experienced the denouement and made my judgments
        and maybe called a friend to share my insights and my acumen.

Not Gus. Gus was just happy being here,
he took it as it came, the sunlight from the east, the sunlight
        from the south, the sunlight from the west.
That was fine for him.

So were the chairs and the sofas and the tables and the terrace —
        oh boy, that hot brick terrace in the summer sun, that was
        good for a good long nap,
and then Gus would be calling at the door and I would let him in
        and he would go to sleep in a cool place for a while.
Then it would be time to eat.

Gus died in his shoebox on the sofa on a Monday afternoon,
        following a stroke on Saturday, and I have to say this:
that dear cat looked like he had gone to sleep.
Yes. Gus had found his nirvana at last.
A softspoken tabby, medium gray, with turquoise eyes and
        an orange nose and a white chin and a creamy belly
        washed with a suggestion of pink.
That was Gus.
Good colors.
Good sleeper.
Good pal.

Why do women do it—
become so beautiful that you want to put them outside, in the snow,
so you can get on with the things that need to be done,
like listening to the radio, and putting catsup on your lima beans,
and manipulating the sitter to let you stay up longer than
     Mother says you can.

It really is too much.
You have to go to the living room with Daddy, and have a
Canada Dry ginger ale while he has his Monongahela Rye,
     because the beauty in your parents' bedroom is too much to handle,
     too confusing,
Mother and Auntie Barbara getting dressed in virtually
     identical dresses,
straight wool, portrait necklines drenched in white lace, and in the
     middle of the lace, right at the cleavage,
(is it proper to do this, treating their bodies like those of movie stars?)
a red jewel on Mother's navy dress, a green jewel on Auntie Barbara's
     black dress, each surrounded by rhinestones,
and once they get the dresses on, and get all their makeup on,
and are so beautiful you want to call the cops, or Cecil B. DeMille,
or maybe Lou Costello—he could stand there and scream—
the women sit on the bed to do each other's nails.

Daddy's down the hall, calling Dee, calling Sister,
calling Denny and Kline will be here any minute,
and here they are, Adelia and Barbara, towels spread across their laps,
leaning in to each other as though they have a secret,

wisps of Mother's brown hair electrified by Barbara's black curls,
flecks of face powder drifting down on their dark bosoms,
the whole room pulsing with perfume and steam
and barely controlled frenzy as,
first Mother to Barbara, then Barbara to Mother,
with a tiny brush, and a tiny bottle, and absolute concentration—
I have been told not to move, not to say a word, you just sit there,
    like a stone—
they turn each other's fingernails scarlet,
the lushest, most edible color in the world,
and I am getting high on the scent of the polish,
and the color of the color, and the beauty of the women—
just a little four-year-old, perched on a pink grosgrain chair.

I tell you, there ought to be a law.
They oughtn't to let little boys see such scenes.
They ought to put me outside in the snow myself, making a
    snowman or just standing around waiting for the Weirs to pull
    up in their car,
but no, oh no, this is one of those wrenching trials of childhood:
I have to stay inside, and watch, and learn, and suffer,
    and try to control myself,
whipped up by the frenzy of the women,
then subdued by their authority,
but for Lord's sake (I certainly agree with Daddy here),
why don't they paint their nails *before* they get dressed?—
why don't they paint their nails *in the afternoon?*—

but they never do,
at the last minute they are always whooping and screeching
    around like banshees,
waving their fingers in the air and getting Daddy to
    put their furs around their shoulders and bending down
    to kiss me good-night with their arms
    thrust back, like angels zooming in for a landing,
and then I am alone, at the window, forlorn as the family dog, watching
    my whole world depart.

However, I recover.
I am young, resilient.
I forget these assaults of beauty and sorrow, get busy with my plans
    for what we will all do on Sunday,
as I grind up graham crackers with Gram's old mortar and pestle, adding
    milk, and—yes, I tell the sitter, always; it helps me sleep—
    drinking down the slop before I go to bed,
all the way down the hall at the back of the apartment,
on the second floor of a tall old house at the top of a hill in Pittsburgh
where the world goes on forever outside my window
and the smelters flare all night.

It's the autumn of 1770,
and the courtesan Handayu of the Nakaomiya house of pleasure
wears a white kimono over scarlet robes.
The obi at her waist is purple, this purple,
the shade of passion
when passion masks despair.

Handayu has been summoned to a party for powerful men.
She loves a man who has no power.
As she hurries from the Nakaomiya house of pleasure,
the lantern carried by her maid illumines flakes of snow.

It's even hard to find in my bag of colors, this pale violet,
snuggled in among the purples and the lavenders
and the grays that go toward red and blue.
I plucked it out, the way one plucks the first violet of spring, .
that tiny flower with almost no stem
nestled down among the leaves like a jewel dropped
    by a forgetful goddess
on her way to meet a god.

Not a big god. Not Zeus or Mars or Vulcan,
none of those macho dudes clanking away at major deeds.

No, let's say Aurora's on her way to meet the god of evening,
the god of winter evenings in Manhattan when the afterglow
    of the sun's descent above the Palisades
    takes on this violet hue,
and Cary Grant in an East River penthouse
starts dressing for a night on the town.

The jewel lies there till spring when Cary and Grace Kelly
    chance to find it as they stroll Central Park in the sun.
He wears a pale blue sweater and a crocus-yellow shirt.
She wears a dress of pale violet and a big straw hat with
    purple ribbons.
She laughs with the sound of coins shaken in a champagne
    glass as she drops the jewel again,
an accidental flower in the fresh green grass.

347

What do you do with a mother who follows the rules?
Who insists on following the rules even when she doesn't
	believe in the rules,
who follows the rules because Grandmother follows the rules,
	and Grandmother is Daddy's mother who lives
	two blocks east of us,
and Grandmother wore widow's weeds for two years following
her husband's death in 1924,
and so now, in 1949, we have Mother in mourning,
Mother going out to work in black and gray to pay off
	the enormous bills that Daddy's dying incurred.
And to keep us going in a house of our own.

No way that we can live at Grandmother's, we all know that,
having lived there every time that Daddy went to hospital and
	Mother drove downtown to be with him.
No way that two young boys, ten and four, are going to put up
	with fingerbowls and portières and prisms and not doing this
	and not doing that until you would think it is we who are
	dead, we who are embalmed in a vault of furnishings,
so for Lord's sake, Mother, can't you relent a little?
Can't you bend the rules?
Can't you wear red once in a while?

Not till May, she declares, but I can't wait for May.
Six feet tall at age ten, I will not wait for May.
Come Christmas 1949 I go to Marshall Field's in Evanston
    and buy an artificial carnation. Red, very satisfactory,
    exactly the right accent for Mother's gray suit or
    her black wool dress.
I want to make this flower irresistible. I want Mother to
    unwrap the box on Christmas morning and cry
    with joy and stick the flower on her robe or
    in her hair or between her teeth. I want her to get up
    and do the fandango.
Yes, I do. I want some life in this house. I want some music
    and some dancing and some horsing around. Some
    nonsense such as Daddy was adept at, but he is dead now,
    in the ground, so what is the sense of Mother getting
    buried, too?
Does she have to act moribund because Grandmother is?

Whereas I am a wizard and I will cast a spell on the flower.
I will make it perfect.
I will make it impossible for Mother not to put on.
I take the carnation to her bedroom, where I douse it with
    Chanel No. 5 and . . .

and it dies.

Right before my eyes the perky flower collapses, becomes a flaccid
    jumble, like a little red dishmop.

No matter what I do, it lies there limp and stupid;

I can't resurrect it and I can't afford another.

I don't know about sizing. No one's ever told me about sizing.

I'm a boy. Boys aren't supposed to know about sizing.

However, the red carnation is dead and I killed it, along with
    Mother's chances to recover from Daddy's death and evade
    the cruel dictates of her mother-in-law and meet
    a man to go dancing with and show off her terrific legs.

As a wizard I'm a failure—and as a horticulturist, too.

The dead carnation is the saddest story I know, much sadder
    than Daddy's death because there was nothing you could
    do about that; sixteen months before he died,
    the surgeon told Mother he was doomed, the cancer had
    spread from his lungs to his spine, and Mother had to go
    around putting a bright face on things. Making plans
    for the future.

Which this dumb flower does not have.

It lolls around in Mother's top drawer for a year or so until
    it disappears, thank God,

and I go on to other endeavors, like puberty. And dreams.

I know I can't get Daddy back so I don't dream
    of him. Daddy is gone.
In the afternoons when I am home from school and Mother
    is at work and Woody's playing in his room and
    the housekeeper's in the kitchen,
I go to Mother's room.
I take out her garnet jewelry and hold it up
    to the window to bring the red lights on.
I put her red high-heeled sandals on my hands and dance them
    on the bed.
At the bottom of her bottom drawer I dig out her Merry
    Widow bra, the one she used to wear with cocktail dresses
    when Daddy was alive. I spread it on the bed with her shoes.
At the cleavage of this lacy black contraption is a
    glowing red jewel—
like the jewel on a dress she used to wear in Pittsburgh,
back when there were four of us, and all of us were fine.

The 350s

I have gone to the drawer for these friends
and fanned them out on the table,
350 so bright that you are wary of using it too often,
and 353, the palest of the shades,
so dear that you ask it to sit down,
fetch a cup of tea for 353,
and speak of the garden in March with the narcissus coming on.

These shades of coral resemble four sisters,
350 the eldest, a big strong girl
who is loving underneath her bossy surface,
concerned for her siblings yet assertive for herself.
She will have three lovers early,
then settle down and raise the kids.

351 and 352 are the sisters who get called each other's names,
wear each other's clothes, trade boyfriends,
travel with the same pack of girls.
One is darker, one is lighter;
together they are sunrise, the glory of the day.

And here, again, is 353, the shade of peachy-pink in the dawn,
a girl so beautiful that no one takes her seriously,
a girl so tender that everybody walks her home,
a girl who blossoms at nineteen,
puts her hair up,
and grinds men's hearts into dust.

Men will dream so often of having loved her,
they will end up believing that they did,
will speak to their friends of that night in Provence,
when her car broke down and she sought refuge at an inn
where the two of them shared a carafe of rosé wine
before they went upstairs,
he carrying her bag,
she carrying her little dog Pepé.

This lavender that's brushed with gray
    recalls the shade of winter afternoons in Pittsburgh
    when I waited for my father to come home.
Oh, there was war out there, and steel mills feeding war,
and diabetic Daddy managing the credit of Carnegie-Illinois Steel
    to do his part—

whereas I at age five was opposed to war.
I was opposed to bloodshed.
I was opposed to little boys growing up to be
    slaughtered in the streets,
or in the air, or on the ocean.
No, I wanted no part of that, which I saw plenty of in Life magazine,
the skies over London red with fire,
and the deep holds of warships red with fire,
and the smelters down by our rivers red with fire,
and Daddy coming home with a suit on and a carton of Camels.

Daddy was winning his war, against rationing,
and I was winning mine, coloring on Hastings Street until my room
    was spring and peace and glory all at once,
happy people in a happy land picking flowers for the ones they loved,
bringing flowers in to place in blue-glass bowls on the sideboard,
glass as blue as the blue vault of heaven, from which no one ever fell
    in fiery spirals,
and no one laid a single flower on a grave.

Take this gold and go to Turkey, to the site of ancient Troy.
In these threads you have it all:
the joy and the sorrow of being human,
of being both magnificent and small—
of being nothing at all before the implacability
 of what will be,
 and be,
 and be,
kingdom upon kingdom in the soils of history.

From Troy, golden vessels of antiquity.
From France, golden threads for embroidery.

And over all, the crashing of the brilliant sea.

This color is calling out to me.
It is calling, "Do not let me go unnoticed, unrecognized, unsung.
I am humble, I am useful,
a color for the earth when the world is leaching out in November
and people start to worry, 'How will we make it through the cold?'"

This color calls,
"I am of the stuff that helps you make it through:
I am of the straw that keeps the winter fields from freezing too deep,
the straw whose sweetness fills the loft
and eases the stalls of the beasts as

"winter works its way into spring
and the green in the meadows starts to take hold,
stalks of asparagus piercing my cover
and strawberries bunching in my cushions as

"the summer grasses rise above me,
grasses so thick and so green
you think that you will never get me back,
nor ever need me,
so strong is the hold of summer on the earth,

"this earth, my earth, to which I return in September,
suntanned and healthy, like a voyageur back from the tropics,
ready to help with the heavy tasks of winter,
with the bedding of the harvest, the birthing of the lambs.

"Oh hold me," calls this pale gold color, "as I hold you."
"Use me," calls this straw, "and we will make it through."

3328

Here is a color that I can't name in one word,
but I use it all the time.
I use it for red when the sun has turned a corner,
I use it for coral when evening's coming on.
It is friendly to pinks from the border of orange,
and with browns it really comes alive,
sets up housekeeping and asks the yellows in for tea.

But get this: 3328 is just as friendly with the reds
     and the blues.

I tell you, this is a color for all seasons,
the perfect candidate for student-body president.
It's always straightforward, reasonable,
says hi to everybody in the halls.
It's even been known to wear the same outfit
     twice in one week!

Oh boy. I might suspect this color is a phony—
if it weren't so doggone sweet.

3607

I have to admit I'm suspicious of this color.
Wary, even though I've come to use it a lot.
For one thing, if my daughter were going to the prom,
I would not select this fuchsia for her gown.
On the other hand, she might.

I mean, here we are, the kind of folks
who button up the house by ten,
having guaranteed
    that the dog has been walked
    that the cat has come in
    that the African violets have been watered
    that the basement lights are off.
And all the while we are doing our duty,
tucking in the little ones and saying our prayers,
3607 is out at the roadhouse,
dancing the Monkey with a man named Earl!

What do you do with a color like this?
Lock her up?
Take away her ankle bracelet?
Make her enroll in data-entry?
No, you old stuffed shirt, just let her be,
soaring on her wings of neon
to the lipstick chorus line.

3685

Say you see it in a store, in a dress, this red, you could well say,
    "Too dark" and pass it by.

But you come back.
You have to come back.
This red calls out your name.

It may take days for you to hear the call, seeing the kids
    through the flu,
or working on the annual report,
or traveling to California,
but one day you know.
It hits you so hard and so fast—while you are
    making orange juice,
or reviewing the notes to the financial statements,
or having lunch with a high-school friend—that,
as soon as you can get there, as soon as you can get away,
    as soon as it's okay to leave,
you head for the store,
fingers crossed that the dress is still there, that it hasn't been
    sold, that they can order it again, that you can take another
    size, that even as you stand there bereft of all the dresses in
    that shade in the store, a woman brings one back,
    and it fits you just fine.

This red is a sleeper because it seems to go toward both blue
    and brown without being purple or maroon.
It's the red of young burgundy, a wine that will age well, and
    you buy new makeup for the shade.

If you don't have diamonds, rhinestones will do.
Lots of rhinestones.
Without a moment's hesitation when you are wearing this red,
you stand up at a party and belt out a song.

"Yesterday." "Heart Like a Wheel." "Milord."

In this red you are an unexpected star.

3750

When I was a little boy
    I had a storybook about the making of a suit,
a blue suit for a boy who lived in the country on a farm.
His father sheared the wool for the suit from the sheep,
then his mother carded the wool, and spun it,
and dyed it in a vat of indigo.
She hung the hanks of wool on a line
    where they turned the green grass blue as they dried.
Then she wove this blue wool into worsted
    and sewed a suit from the cloth for her son.

Hello, 3750.
The last time we met I was sitting beside Mother,
looking at the pictures while she read me that story.
The first grownup suit I had was blue,
and I wore it to Miss Pocock's Dancing Class,
with white cotton gloves and a blue and red silk tie.
My ears stuck out.
My pompadour was carefully arranged.
I never thought of the contribution of sheep
    to my stylish appearance.
I was learning the foxtrot and the rumba and the Charleston.
I was on my way to being Fred Astaire
    and I had no patience with the basics of life.

Thus sons leave the farms
for newfangled lives in the cities.
Thus aging men put their feet up
as they consider the joys of long ago.

3777

Here we have the color of Katharine Hepburn's hair
when the sun at noon in Venice slants down from the south
and the lights along the canal switch on to illuminate
     her *Summertime* plunge.
Yes, Hepburn is the only red haired star in Hollywood who does
     her own stunts,
some of which have not been recorded on film.

I took Hepburn for a walk once and we got lost in the woods and
the owner of the woods came barging out to chastise the carousers
whose violation of community standards his keen ears had
detected among his trees and his trillium and his mertensia and
his wild geranium, for it was spring.

"It's . . . Katharine Hepburn!" he declared.
"Yes!" she replied.
Transferring her brass-topped walking stick to her left hand,
turning on the lights of her legend with her smile,
Hepburn advanced on the landlord with her right hand outstretched.
"We've just been poaching in your woods."

"You can poach in my woods any time," the landlord replied as he
     shook her hand.
But Hepburn and I were off to the lake, on the path the landlord
     pointed out, and his dog came along, and we had a good time,
     talking about our families and throwing sticks for the dog and
     enjoying the day.

Hepburn wore a black silk turtleneck, navy wool shirt, tan trousers,
     brown boots.
No green.
It was all about us in the woods, though. On the trees and the saplings
     and the bushes and the flowers, there was every shade of green
     that you have ever seen—
and then this rich red hair
cherishing the sun in the sweet May air.

3824

The second time that she got married, Mother wore this peachy shade,
and I was so glad to see her go.
I was so tired of the responsibility of looking after her
and being her main man,
even though I wasn't and could never be.
There I was at thirty-three, a little kid again,
kicking up his heels that Mommy was gone, gone at last,
long gone, well gone, to Florida,
leaving her older son free to be he.

Which didn't happen for a long time,
but that doesn't matter.
What matters now, in 1973, is that Mother is she,
a wife again, in her husband's house on Siesta Key,
and Lowell is Daddy's cousin and he remembers Grandfather Beal,
the first Wood Beal, come alive for his grandsons at last,
strolling through his days with his wife Mary Ellen,
who drove him mad the way she drove the rest of us mad,
with her fingerbowls and fol-de-rol and fussy French words.

Adelia has brought us into life again, which is all that you can ever ask
    of a mother,
bringing us around a table, Lowell and she and Woody and me,
    Joan and Augie and Bob and Barb and Cynny,
a lot of people together at last, a family together, with a real
    acknowledged head,
not three offshoots shooting off,
looking for ways out of selfishness and loneliness and not being whole,
and not finding a way because they keep being apart.

No matter that she died.
Adelia quested to the end, driving out for vegetables far
    out in the country,
driving out for the best vegetables that she could buy,
    true quality vegetables, the kind you would be proud to
    serve to the Junior League,
and getting hit to death by some baseball players' car.

No matter any of the pain. Mother brought us back in.
She proved that there was more to life than Daddy's death. Or hers.
She proved that you keep going no matter what.

This is a gray that tells us we are loved,
that the world is safe, that everything will be all right.
This is the gray of the shadows in the black-and-white rooms
  where Margaret O'Brien slept,
the rooms perfect sets of rooms and Margaret's pigtails
  perfect on the pillow as she relaxed into sleep from her last big scene,
as she became just another kid who will make it through the night.

A warm gray, a friendly gray, almost a showoff gray,
a gray that will walk down the street for red,
a gray that encourages all the red in browns.
I have seen these colors come together in "Mystery Train,"
a film in which the bellhop Cinqué Lee wears a suit of 414,
and the night manager Screamin' Jay Hawkins
  wears a scarlet outfit—
Yes, scarlet! Scarlet coat and scarlet tie and scarlet shirt,
  plus lots of big gold rings—
and the rich brown skin of these men makes
  the gray and scarlet sing.
Thrum. The colors thrum,
while Screamin' Jay's bright rings play timpani,
and my eighty eyes go dancing like Rockettes.

One summer night in Winnetka, 414 walked over from next door
  to greet the folks at Ray and Ellen's barbecue.
The cat was a plump old Russian blue named Beau
and he resembled an amiable banker in a three-piece flannel suit
  as he strolled from group to group and held his head up to be stroked.

Take this gray home.
Hold it in your hands.
You can feel its heart beat through the skein.

498

Okay, all right, I confess:
I would dress as a woman to wear this red.
I would put it all on, wig and makeup and padding,
lingerie and nylons and three-inch heels,
just to enter a room in this red.
And knock them dead.

I tell you, this color smacks of sacrifice,
all the way back to entrails in the Roman sun,
and all the way forward to the film "Ménage"
in which Gerard Depardieu ends up in drag, for love,
and that's why I would wear a dress of 498—for love:
for love of the color, this bright ruby red,
and for love of all the men undone when I stroll in,
a gardenia in my ash-blonde hair,
a cigarette in a holder in my gloved hand,
a smile of triumph on my glossy lips
because I have succeeded in wearing more of this red than
    any man is ever allowed to wear red, red all the way
    from my shoulders to my knees,
and because I am splendid in this splendid rig.

Oh yes, they will all cluster round me,
offering to light my cigarette, offering to smoke my cigarette,
    offering to transport the heavy holder to my lips,
offering to fetch me a daiquiri, a diamond bracelet, a fortune in
    securities, the Empire State Building in my name,

these solicitous swains played by Clark Gable and
    William Holden and Laurence Olivier,
these hesitant shyguys played by Humphrey Bogart and
    Gary Cooper and Harpo Marx (who regards me like a
    transfixed sheep),
these Roman emperors played by Claude Rains and
    Sir Cedric Hardwicke and Louis Calhern,
each one willing to go the limit to accompany me through life,
each one representing a match made in heaven which,
by the end of the evening, I am forced to decline—

having fallen in love myself with Marlene Dietrich—
whose long red nails are longer and redder than mine,
whose glossy red lips are glossier and redder than mine,
whose will to succeed will not be quenched, not for love,
not for lust, not for the gardenia from my hair,
Dietrich in her railroad flat the next evening calling in
    the 1950s cops to arrest me for a deviant,
then swinging out the door *in my red dress!* to cook up crimes
    with Richard Widmark in a nightclub where the ceiling is low and
    the lights are dim and Dietrich, *still in my red dress!*,
    gets up to sing "Smoke Gets in Your Eyes" while
    back at the precinct house I am trying to explain to
    Sergeants Murphy and O'Brien what love for a color
    can do to a guy,

WHEREUPON, it being the night of the Policeman's Ball, and
    Murphy and O'Brien being dateless,
we speed to Lowdown Lou's where the cops arrest
    Dietrich and Widmark for theft of my red dress,
    after which I wear it to the ball and dance all night with
    Pat and Mike, Pat's gardenia in my hair, Mike's gardenia
    on my wrist, and on my legs stockings I have stripped
    from Dietrich, black Schiaparellis with a clock on each
    calf in the shape of a dagger, and on my bosom a diamond
    Cupid's arrow that Widmark stole from Tiffany.

Oh yes, this red turns any man into a femme fatale, and any
    woman, too,
so Watch Out, World:
498 is the red that can make
an utter fool of you.

Here is a color you can never take away from me.
It made a hole in my eyes when I was young,
and now my eyes gather round its memory like deer around a pool,
lapping at the beauty of this rich magenta,
a red that persists like the beat of my heart.

I can still feel the color in my hands,
lengths of bunchy dry chiffon that had tied around the waist
      of a pale blue pleated evening gown, also chiffon,
but one I never saw, the gown and its sash having been reduced to
      scraps in a box in Mother's bottom drawer by the time
      I got around to looking for salvation on my own
      and finding it in colored cloth.

My heart is still sore I never saw the hat
      that Auntie Barbara wore when she married Uncle Ned.
They eloped to his parents' home in Iowa, and Barbara, who was
      so beautiful she took your breath away,
who made men walk into walls and say dumb things,
who was tall and shapely like a goddess,
with black eyes and black curls and the sweet precise features of
      a pampered cat—
Barbara when she raised her starry lashes and said I do to Ned
wore a black velvet hat—she told me this, several times—
trimmed with pale blue satin and American Beauty velvet.

Wow! Holes in my heart and holes in my eyes.
I was much too young to marry Barbara her second time around—
      Uncle Jimmy got her then,
and I never felt comfortable dancing with Mother,
but each of these tall, dark-haired, dark-eyed women remains
      triumphant in my mind,
each in red and blue, in magenta and pale blue,
the colors of the dawn of a little boy's love.

Blanc
Neige

It is 1947, spring, and Dr. Ida Maria Hamilton Laird Barroll
    is walking down the street.
In Washington, D.C.
Retired from her obstetrics/pediatrics practice in Winnetka, Illinois,
she has moved to K Street with her husband Henry, who is
    working for the government.

Dr. Barroll knows everything she needs to know about
    everything that matters,
and if that man across the street doesn't get to a doctor soon,
he will be dead. Congestive heart failure.
Goiter, Dr. Barroll observes to a woman in a silver fox jacket.
Phthisic, she says to a woman in blue waiting for a bus.
Fresh lesions, she says to a man coughing into his sleeve
    outside a coffee shop.
Love, she says to a couple walking arm in arm before her.

White, says Dr. Barroll that evening as she sits at her
    dressing table to brush her hair.
Blanc neige, she says, remembering the embroidery floss with which
    her oldest daughter Dee has smocked dresses for the daughters of
    her younger daughters Betty and Jean,
and those granddaughters, Ida understands as she brushes, will have
    daughters, too,
and their hair will go gray, and their hair will go white,
and they will love their husbands and they will love their work and
    they will love their children,
and while they brush their hair when they are old,
they will think that it has all been worth it,
    all the suffering and making do and getting by,
the being a woman in a man's world and a man's profession—
and what on earth did it matter so long as she worked hard and
    saved lives?

Life was the issue, right from the beginning,
and Dr. Barroll is proud that she could serve.

There. That's it.
Having done her hair in a twist, she anchors it in place with
a blue velvet bow.
Not bad for an old girl, she thinks as she leaves the apartment to
meet Henry at the scallop house across the street from the
mansion of Evalyn Walsh McLean, who owns the Hope diamond,

a stone as blue as the blue velvet bow in Ida's blanc neige hair.

613

She has been alone this summer
while her husband drives a wagon train west.

Although he smiles, and tips his hat, and bustles back and forth,
showing her the goods from his wagon,
the peddler who has stopped at the sod house
is not a pleasant man.

Across the prairie, the sky takes on this shade of
thunderstorm yellow.

Her children have walked into town.

640

Every now and then, when I open up the drawers where
  I keep my bags of floss,
I wonder, will I end up doing a poem for each shade?
Will I end up in the old folks' home, feeble and cross, squawking
    that they can't take my leg off, or root out my arteries,
    or remove my gizzard till I do the last three shades that
    DMC manufactures?

Whereupon the company announces twelve more shades—
and I just die, exasperated that the rich variety of life
    has kept me from accomplishing my task,
has left me high and dry like old Odysseus,
washed up at the end of his line, on Ithaca,
looking out on the seas he has traveled and
    the islands he has visited,
each one a dot of color in a field of changing blues.

But anywhere Odysseus went was okay with him,
and that's the way it is with me,
holding in my hands a skein, and thinking where it takes me,
and then just going—just going off,
maybe all the way to places I have never been but understand
    because I hold the color in my hand,
or going many places all at once, seeing in a skein of taupe
    desert mountains north of Las Vegas last summer,
    and Mother's winter coat in the 1950s,
    and the flesh of a puffball we found in the woods in 1968
    and took back home to fry.

These skeins are magic carpets for my mind, and for my heart,
Mother's brown wool coat with the black velvet collar
    wet with snow when she comes home from the office,
the Nevada mountains hot and dusty, flashing their striations like
    lightning bolts,

and the big white puffball risen from the woods floor
    like a happy shmoo, offering itself to be eaten and enjoyed—

and now, in my hands, the color 640 journeying
    across my canvas in the stitching of a crate on Lady Watanabe's
    bamboo raft as she sails from Tokyo to Pittsburgh to retrieve her
    purloined fan.

Do you know this?
In Pittsburgh during World War II (Daddy told me the story in
    Schenley Park one day),
there was a movement to uproot the ginkgo trees presented to the city
    in the 1930s by the emperor of Japan.
The Japanese had bombed Pearl Harbor. We would kill their trees.
Daddy was happy to report this movement failed,
and I am happy too.
Now I keep a Pittsburgh ginkgo leaf on my shelves.
Now I say, Hot dog!
Go, Pirates!
Go, Ralph Kiner!
Go, Lady Watanabe!
Go, Carnegie-Illinois Steel!
Go, ginkgo trees!

Nothing will die, or not come back, or not endure forever,
if you love it enough.
Love is the key.
Ask Odysseus.
Ask Telemachus.
Ask Penelope.

I roam the rooms of my memory,
the way I looked through Daddy's wardrobe as a kid,
and I cannot find a single color to associate with the man.
Not a real color.
Nothing for my eyes to seize and float to safety on.

The suits in Daddy's wardrobe are gray,
and the ties that hang on a metal rack inside the door
    are maroon and navy, colors to tie up the dog with,
and his socks are maroon and navy, plus gray and black,
and on weekends when he's taking it easy,
he wears a tan sleeveless sweater or his old dark purple Williams sweater,

but he did not live long enough to blossom out
    in pink in the fifties (pink shirts were all the rage in 1952,
    with pink and black ties).
No. Daddy died in 1949, of cancer, at age thirty-nine,
and when I got confirmed I wore an old tie of his,
maroon and ultramarine, with a pattern like lopsided Easter eggs,
    but I didn't like that tie. I didn't wear it again.
Its memory gives me the willies.

I wore his sweaters for a while but they were old and dull,
and the stone in his ring that I still wear is dark red and dull,
and I want to say, Daddy, dear Daddy, this man
    who did not live long enough to become Dad or Father or Pop,
this man who is stuck in the amber of my childhood,
almost young enough when he died to be my son today,

I want to ask him, I want to know, what color was yours?

Blue or green, I suspect, or blue and green together,
the colors of a happy brook.
The color of laughter.
All day long in Pittsburgh, Mother and I would do our duties, me being

smart and good, she being tasteful and industrious,
      storing up homemade jam and homemade chili sauce and
      clean curtains and suitable invitations against
      Daddy's return,
he coming in from work, and getting his drink, and sitting
      down to read the paper with his gold watch chain
      stretched across his forehead, penknife over one ear,
      watch over the other, Daddy reading the paper and
      drinking Monongahela Rye and smoking Camel cigarettes
      and looking like a balding Sheherazade in his chair,
      all dolled up to go dancing while he follows the war.

This is it. That's my father. A tall thin handsome man
      who doesn't care one whit about the job he has to go to do,
who just goes out and does it the way that mules haul grindstones,
getting his picture in the business section, and being proposed
      for the University Club, and getting a pain in his arm,
      and finding out it is cancer in his lung,
cancer that spreads to his spine, Daddy lying in the front
      bedroom of our house on Greenwood Street in Evanston,
      where we have moved after Pittsburgh, Daddy in a hospital bed,
      legs paralyzed, laughing till the tears come over something silly
      his mother has said.

"What is that, Son?" she inquires after he has had his shot.
"Morphine, Mother."
"Careful, Son. You'll get addicted."
"Mother. I *am* addicted."

And off she goes back home, Mary Ellen Nutt Beal in her red Miss Edythe hat, and her black wool coat with the black persian-lamb sleeves, and her white gloves, and her black pocketbook, a transplanted Southerner, a stranger in a strange land, appalled by the depths to which her son has sunk, she should have known something was wrong when he started losing his hair, such a beautiful baby, such beautiful golden curls.

I'm wrong. Daddy's color is gold,
pure gold,
and I am very proud of him.

It's World War II, and Ingrid Bergman wears
    to the Academy Awards
a gown of buttercup yellow, this soft sunny shade.
The gown has rhinestone straps, almost no back,
and Bergman as she strides across the stage
    of the Pantages Theater holds her shoulders straight to keep
    the straps in place.
She walks with vigor, purpose,
and the only way that you can tell she's dined too well
    is that her smile stays on so long and she fusses with her hair.

Stromboli is ahead of her, the postwar affair with Rossellini,
the violence of seaside love, the virulence of stateside gossip,
the triumphant return.

For now, in America, we are getting restless with the war.
The tide in the Pacific has turned
    and we are sensing we can win.
In our kitchen in Pittsburgh I am helping Mother out,
kneading the orange dot in the plastic bag of white margarine,
yellowing the substance into butter's lookalike.

The color matches Mother's hat of water lilies,
big smooth white petals, shaggy buttercup centers.
When Mother is out and Ora is in,
I wear this hat with the red skirt from my Beloved Belindy doll
and I ride the Hoover upright that Ora pushes round the rooms.
Ora calls me Stephen Horse Mouse Pumpkin Beal,
which is okay with me,
though the chairs and tables I acknowledge as we pass
know me by much finer names:

The King of Linden Avenue;
something on the order of . . .
Stromboli Beal.

Ah well, what else is life about but the chance to dream good
　　　dreams?
I thought that I'd end up as Stewart Granger—
Jimmy Stewart at the least,
but here I am, and there I was,
a flashy comic in bad drag waving from a vacuum cleaner:
Baby Milton Berle.

A long way out there, at the very base of the horizon,
the point at which Lake Michigan becomes
    the rest of the world,
reducing Savannah and Gibraltar, Athens and New Delhi,
    Tokyo and San Francisco into one thin line —
that line is pure energy,
that line is this sizzling white,
this yellow crackling out in the shade of lightning bolts,
then coalescing as the rising winter moon.

Here's a conundrum:
746 is 747, except it is not blue.
Tweed these colors together and they don't turn green.
They are simply a transition of air,
blending upward from the world beyond the horizon
    to the sky that holds you in.

Most people never even see 746,
but it is always here,
radiating off the cornfields at midday in July,
streaking across a Venetian interior by John Singer Sargent,
a dark shadowed space where people gather,
riven by the grace of God.

747

Here is the shade of the early morning air
at the point on the horizon where the world goes on forever.
Here is your pale blue entry into neverendingness,
the wings on which the everlasting sails.

Other colors drive into town, go shopping,
buy jeans for the kids or kibble for the dog.
Other colors sweat and swink their way through life,
staying mindful of relationships with others,
responsibilities, the mutual supports of shade and hue.

Whereas 747, because it goes with everything,
is blithe.
It will never steer you wrong, this blue;
it will never take over—and it will never disappear.
Wherever you place this blue on your canvas,
it behaves like an angel, blessing all about it
        with equanimity, with purity,
with the unassuming grace of the beloved.

This blue is the blue of everything that you aspire to,
and everything that you hold dear.
More than any blue I know,
this blue is clear.

She alights from the cab like Venus from a barque,
her toddler daughter beside her, an attendant cherub.
Hastings Street starts at the bottom of the hill,
where the shops are, and it ends at the top of the hill,
at the corners I am not allowed to cross,
and here is Auntie Barbara more than halfway up the hill,
but down a long flight of stairs from our house,
framed by the snow and the trees and the street and the houses
    across the street,
a beauty canted for ascension yet standing still.

The little boy comes down the stairs—
forever, it seems; it seems that he will never get there—
yearning to ascertain that this woman is real,
yearning to be hugged,
yearning to be incorporated into her universe—

and then he is with her,
with the flesh and the fur and the silk and the wool,
with the perfume and the lipstick and the powder,
with the sparkling black eyes and the curly black hair,
with all this exquisite substance warmly embracing him,
and through it all he is hearing a new sound,
a bright fresh sound,
a clinking, chinking sound,
like morning ice breaking on an early spring lake.

Auntie Barbara's hat is made of porcelain roses,
cold to the touch, pale pink to the eyes,
and in the place where this little boy dwells,
half substance, half imagination,
a globe of his own girded about with the thin gold wires of rules,
he understands that God has made this hat for his aunt,
that its breakability protects her from harm,

that she will never suffer and never know pain
    so long as she is as she is,
a beauty wearing beauty for beauty's sake,
a willing subject of her great success,
an eager participant in the joy that she imparts.

Thus I come down the hill to be embraced by beauty,
then turn around and trudge back up the hill to duty,
to home, to school, to being good, to not touching
    Auntie Barbara's hat,
or dragging her sables around by their tails,
or playing in the basement coal with my cousin.
I come back up the hill to all the stuff of being a kid and
    growing up and learning my lessons and not talking back,

but I also know this—
deep down at the heart of my being I know this:

I have taken part in beauty and beauty never dies.
There is something that transcends anything
    that I can ever learn at home or in school,
and that is what is.

Forever in the world—
of this I am sure: forever—
a beautiful black-haired woman will be standing in the
    Pittsburgh snow,
wearing a hat of porcelain roses,
cold to the touch, pale pink to the eyes.

762

I can be stitching along on a canvas,
needing a shade that holds the light without getting hot,
and 762 will come to mind.

I am always grateful for this gray.
I take it from my plastic bag of grays feeling good about my choice,
the way that Humphrey Bogart, private eye,
would select a linen suit for a busy summer day:
morning spent on a case, then lunch at the track,
followed by the afternoon trifecta.

With his pale gray suit Bogie wears a lavender shirt,
    a navy polka-dot foulard.
His hat's a cream Panama, banded with navy,
and the camera follows the races through reflections
    in his sunglasses, smoked gray with gold rims,
the horses thundering across his temples toward Alexis Smith,
who has plans for him that afternoon.

Bogie's boxers are blue broadcloth,
too full for his bony frame,
and you can see a wet patch at the base of his singlet
    as he leans over to unsnap his garters
    just as Alexis fires.

"So you're the one who killed the Countess!" he declares.

Alexis in a peach satin slip is weeping.
"This doesn't mean that I don't love you," she responds,
then blows her brains out on the bed that would have
    marked the start of her redemption,
had she not loved money more.

What do you say about a gray that goes to bloodbaths
    and comes out looking spiffy every time?
"Customary cool," the morning Eagle blares.
In the front-page photo, Bogie stands
    on the sidewalk with the cops, turning to light a cigarette as
    the medics wheel his lady love away.

817

This is the red that you get serious over,
the one, when you see it,
you understand you have been waiting for,
the red that's it,
the one you know you can make love to
　　the rest of your life.

Oh, sure, there may be times when orange reds look better,
those cheerleader shades bouncing around in the snow.
In softer lights you may be seduced by purple reds,
but something in their nature has other ideas,
wants to study with a guru or write a novel about pain.

We might as well be grown-up about this.
There are times you will want the deeper reds,
the darker reds, the burgundies that lead you
　　down to the waterfront where nights never end.
Now and then, to your surprise,
you will be taken by the sweet obligers,
the pinks in tasteful blouses
　　who offer second helpings of what was not enough to start.

But you'll come back.
You will not be able to stay away.
817 is the red that you are wed to
　　because it always works.
This red will always delight you,
and always support you,
and always strut down the street like
Marilyn Monroe.

Life got better when I could wear red ties.

I would like to say that I was smart right from the beginning,
that I wore to Miss Pocock's Dancing Class every Friday after
     junior high
a succession of red ties that inflamed the girls with ardor and
chagrined the boys with envy.

No such luck.
Like most of us caught in our time, I got along in blue ties with
     some red,
and when I went to college and Mother wasn't there,
I bought a yellow challis paisley at The House of Walsh.

Yes, I did. Yellow—
and I wore this tie with a blue Brooks Brothers oxford-cloth
     button-down and a brown Brooks Brothers herringbone jacket,
and I will say this for the kid that I was then: I looked pretty
     good in that outfit.
I was dressed in the fashion of Professor Whitney Stoddard who
     taught art and knew everyone and had been in Daddy's
     class as his son was in my class,
and so yellow was all right.
You hear that, Mother? Yellow was sanctioned. At Williams.
Yellow would do.

I also wore this outfit down to New York City
where its splendor inflamed
     not only women but men and on one notable
     occasion me.
Sylvia and I had had a fight, again, about doing it, again,
and so there I was in a semi-gay saloon on Third Avenue
     where the men looked me over and I essayed not to notice,
     leaning nonchalantly into the bar with a cigarette and a
     scotch and soda and an acrid smell in the air.

"Excuse me, sir" the bartender said. "You are burning your hair."
"Thank you," I replied, ever in control.
Nonchalantly, I removed the cigarette from my temple
    and patted down the burn, then went to the men's room
    for a breather.
The plump man who fondled me also alarmed me,
so back I went to Sylvia, and unguent, and another
    fruitless night in her roommate's bed while her roommate
    slept with her.

I had my first red tie in the sixties, real red, red challis,
    with some gold and taupe doodads, and I wore it a lot,
but I still wasn't smart enough to know that if this stalwart man was
    going to be he, always he, truly he, he was going to wear red
    around his neck every chance he got.
Oh, the chances I let go, let slip by my grasp like autumn leaves
    on a river, like the smile of a stranger through the window
    of a passing train, like that plump guy on Third Avenue,
    who looks sort of cute from this distance, but he is gone now, too,
    utterly gone,
gone like the blue ties and the burgundies, the occasional green tie and
    the yellows, the plaids and the reps and the paisleys, all gone,
now it's only red, red the few times I wear a tie,
because now it's only jeans for work.
Now, when I am duded up, I wear a red silk tie from Field's, scarlet,
    with diagonal stripes of black and white polka-dots.
I wear a carmine silk patterned with Marilyn Monroe.
    From T. J. Maxx.

I wear a-lotta-red-with-a-little-white-and-blue cotton for the
     Fourth of July, from Bill,
and when the occasion requires evening dress, every five years or so,
     I wear a red kimono with the rest of the tuxedo.

I tell you, Mother, this is war.
No, this is victory. (Mother's dead. I ain't.)
Every time that I walk out in red in the nineties,
I am walking out in yellow in the fifties,
and for now, for a while, I've got a little window of me
     before the seasons and the years close in
     and something or other, grief or fear or illness,
maybe all three, forces me to be careful and proper and dull,
arriving for functions in a gray flannel suit from Field's and
     a blue rep tie from Brooks and—
and a gunnysack over my head!

I'll be dead before I wear that outfit, flat-out croaked,
and I tell you all, I tell my family and friends,
I tell my lovers and my former lovers and concerned passersby:
Don't let them do it!
You lay me out in red and close the coffin fast before some
     tasteful Junior Leaguer ascertains I won't do.

I will do. I do do.
Thank you.

815

Every now and then I need another red.

I know I need it, I tell myself I need it,
I tell myself, It's time you stopped using 817,
it's time you showed your versatility by using other reds,
it's time you showed some scope and some vision—
some mature breadth—
and after all this cogent advice, this disciplined self-talk,
I end up schlepping off with a skein of 817,
because it works,
because I love it,
because I took it from the bag without looking at the label
    and the color in my hand turned out to be:
817 again.

However, this is 815's poem.

When 817 is busy, or washing her hair,
or just in one of her moods,
I take out her sister and we get along just fine.
Her older sister, her darker sister,
her, well, juicier sister, more full figured,
a woman who is earning life by not keeping score.

Oh boy. This is the color of Scarlett's gown the night she goes
    to Ashley's birthday party.
Remember that scene?
Rhett has dressed his wife. He's taken out the gown from her closet,
wine red, a clear burgundy, velvet, with spangles
    round the shoulders,
a harlot's gown for The Woman Who Has Kissed Another Man,

and Scarlett in this red spangled number
stands in the doorway of Ashley's pokey little house
while the women of the town tsk-tsk-tsk her
    up and down,
and Melanie, the ever-forgiving, ever-understanding,
ever-annoying Melanie,
comes beaming over to welcome Scarlett in.
Melanie's in gray, a nice gray, a sweet gray,
with a nice sweet snood on her hair,
and Scarlett just stands there, in the doorway,
dark hair curling to her shoulders,
bosom pulsing in spangles,
a woman who is growing up, in red.

I tell you, I'll be eighty-five or ninety,
and some young thing will pass me by.
Her hair will be dark and long, her dress will be this ruby red,
and I will be dead.
Nothing else for it. Felled by red.
Back at the home, the old folks will gossip
    how this one last gasp of gusto did me in:
"Oh yes, there he was in the park, perched on his bench,
and his gnarled old pecker rose and threw him to the ground."

Oh folks, dear folks, you do not understand.
It was not lust that felled me.
It was delight,
the right color at the right time,
a visit—and a summons—from God.

I probably shouldn't say this, but I will:
You don't have to worry about blue.
Get the value right and the shade will follow,
and if you don't like it, lots of others will.

Take, for instance, your canny academics.
They can always explain a blue, justify a blue,
convince a classroom of students, who would rather be in bed,
    or in Florida, or in something moving fast,
that the blue you didn't get around to fixing
    is the very blue that you intended—
and a master stroke at that.

Take, for instance, Professor Glendenning Vaughan,
late of this world, and of an extensive collection of Harris Tweed jackets
    from which his widow D'Etta is fashioning keepsake quilts
    for the grandchildren—
Vaughan said about the sky in an early Fenstermacher
(it was Monday, April 16, 1962, ten-forty in the morning),
"This blue will do!"

Whereas Fenstermacher himself, at the very moment Vaughan
    clicked in his slide,
was scraping *off* the blue in the selfsame canvas,
which he had filched from his dealer so he could get
    the sky just right,
that pale blue tender Baltic sky at dawn,
and what he had painted in 1951 was too red.

Vaughan sued. So did Fenstermacher's dealer, Benoît of Berne,
Vaughan and Benoît dividing between them the bulk of
    Fenstermacher's oeuvre
(on whose Sotheby auction the Vaughan grandchildren
    are attending college now).

Vaughan and Benoît also got:
  Fenstermacher's collection of Vienna Werkstätte teapots;
  two Pendleton shirts sent to the "paradigmic pasticher"
  (Vaughan's term) by a great-niece in Corvallis
  (Vaughan took the blue plaid, Benoît the red checks);
  and a note from Hildegarde Neff explaining to Fenstermacher
  why she could not come for tea.

Now this is a long way around to saying, Stick to your blue and
  be happy.
If it's 827, don't pull it out for 828. Wait. The sky will be peaceful
  as it is.
As for 519, you need never worry.
With 519 it is always a sunny day,
  in America,
and if you are stitching a Mediterranean sky, say the rising
  of a zeppelin over Marseille harbor, you will want to use 597,
and as the zeppelin keeps rising toward the empyrean,
you will want to shade to 807 and 806, beyond which neither you
  nor the zeppelin will probably go, Zeus being up there, and
  the North Wind, and Judge Crater, and Eleanor Roosevelt, and
  Billie Holliday, and Patsy Cline,
the ladies wearing red-rose corsages on their black evening
  gowns and singing the "St. Louis Blues,"
which are darker and deeper, and not what I mean here.

What I mean here are the blues that you can skate on,
  and swim in, and soar to the sky through on your way to
  being happy all the time,
and if that sounds unrealistic, and unacademic,
and totally outside the great Western tradition of misery,

this fool says, So be it.
He says, Hot dog!
He says, Jesus Loves Me,
and so does Buddha, and so does Yahweh, and so does Allah,
and so does the great god Pan.

He says Man,
he says Woman,
Get a hold on joy.

What we've got here is Spencer Tracy brown.
Just brown.
A brown that goes to work and a brown that hoes the carrots and
    a brown that helps little old nuns cross the street.
Good old brown, as in dogs, as in curls, as in tweeds, as in brogans.
Pat it, comb it, brush it, shine it:
it's all cleaned up,
but it's still brown—

brown roaming off across the hills in the morning,
brown ambling home at night,
sucking at a pipe as it knocks the dirt off its boots,
opens the door and calls that it's home.

Oh sure, she thinks. Brown.
She's spent the afternoon dreaming of aqua . . . aubergine . . . bisque,
intricate colors, splendid ones to bring the magic on,
and what she's got instead is brown,
brown again,
brown as in stew, brown as in bread, brown as in tea—
all the good homey things that make their lives all right.

He takes her in his arms.
She feels his strength.

What does she need with some fop?

I

In his chambers in his town house in Edo,
    the warrior Watanabe Saburo is concluding his career.
He has fought in the summer and winter battles at Osaka.
He has served his emperor well.
Now it is time to take the long road to the hills
    where he will spend his days in contemplation,
tending a garden and keeping some pigs.

In his chambers Watanabe is supervising
    the packing of his gowns for donation to the Nakamura Theater,
where generations of actors will strut his pomp through scenes
    he has not known, and cannot dream of,
being so far removed from pomp in the hills,
with his millet and his onions and his pigs.

The last gown his servants pack is one of brown mulberry,
embroidered across the right shoulder with a branch
    of flowering plum
and along the hem with mounds of melting snow.

Watanabe wore this gown for the funeral of the warlord
    Toyotomi Hideyoshi.
As he took his place in the procession, the smile of a courtesan
    caught his eye.
He did not know her name, or her house;
he did not see her again.

Now, as a servant folds the snowy hem across the flowers,
Watanabe recalls her smile as she raised her fan.

It is all concluded, and it is all beginning,
this great warrior's great quest for joy.

II

They will chatter. They will pose.
They will strut back and forth in his chamber at Versailles
    like a pack of actors performing a farce by Molière.
His sons fatigue him. His nephews fatigue him.
The friends of his sons and his nephews fatigue him.
By the time these fools get it figured out,
which outfits will be whose,
or which outfits they will share,
the outfits will be out of style and the fools will be
    running off to their tailors to learn which scraps of cloth
    may be employed again.

The Count Pierre Chrétien Bertrand Marie de Montalembert
    is retiring to his farm in the south.
He is looking forward to his pigs.
He is looking forward to walking out in the morning with
    a bucket of slops that the pigs will greet with deep grunts
    of satisfaction as they surge along the fence.

Now, at Versailles, the Count regards a young courtier,
one of the friends, a dark-haired fellow in the Count's plum
    breeches and beribboned scarlet heels.
He is playing at dancing the gavotte with the Count's son
    Michel, who wears the plum doublet.
To the Count's old eyes, these boys in their swank
resemble dancing pigs.

Oh yes, it is time for the farm. Time for the soil.
Time for the mornings of joy.

924

You see this color in Rousseau,
lurking in the background,
serving as the basis of the jungle,
the point at which all foliage retreats into itself.
Do you dare to enter this world?
Do you dare to stay away?
Here is the mystery of nature,
the green that may be blue,
the blue that may be green,
the trees that may be sea,
the very core of life.

Childe Hassam has used this shade,
and so has Georgia O'Keeffe, her dark eyes hollow
     with delving into the source of the shade, its primal origin,
the ultimate question—is it leaf or is it water?—
the overwhelming answer—it is all.

Here you have the smack of the gunk from which we spring,
     the gross original stew—
and here you also have the shade of the silk on a Philadelphia lady,
a strawberry blonde dancing the quadrille
     at a ball for General Washington.
Her name is Amarantha. When she marries, she will sit to Copley.
On this festive night she wears pink diamonds in her hair.

You will find this shade in every country of the world,
in every culture—and in every dream.
When you close your eyes at night, think of 924,
and you will be gone.

Think of 924.
You are gone.

And then, in the morning, you arise as from the sea,
on the shore of an island where bougainvillea blooms,
where the palpable air is fragrant with gardenia,
and wild pigs scamper through the forests,
snorting with glee.

930

(With a nod to Peter Ustinov's performance as Nero in the film Quo Vadis)

Here is the color I would wear if I were emperor of China,
a deep gray-blue, like granite,
like the underbelly of a thundercloud,
like the eyes of one who has given up hope, to whom I say,
because I am emperor, because I have the power,
because it does not matter,
    not to me,
"Live! Go ahead and live!"—
and on this granite robe, I will have a yellow dragon
    embroidered, deep yellow, rich yellow, thick gummy
    royal yellow, and the scales of this dragon will be limned
    in chartreuse. His eyes will be scarlet.
He will be glory and vengeance and horror all at once.
He will be I.

Wearing this dragon robe,
I will allow a legation of round eyes to travel inland
    instead of having them put to death;
I will allow my first son to take a fourth wife
    without having the third wife put to death;
I will attend the official celebration of my birthday,
    a fireworks extravaganza extending from midnight to dawn,
    after which I will not have put to death any courtier who
    falls asleep
because it may also happen that my own eyes close—
but only for surcease from the wonder in my thunder-dragon robe.

I tell you, I will admire this robe so much that—
yes, oh yes, this is the correct decision;
this is the wisdom for which history will extol me—
I will *not* have the robe made.

Do you hear that, you sniveling courtiers?
The robe will not be made.

Ah, such is the cunning of the emperor of China,
such is the exquisite sensibility of this mighty ruler
    who hears the nightingales singing in Japan,
    who smells the incense burned to his adoration in Sichuan,
    who tastes the tea of infidels from beyond
        the western mountains,
    and strokes the fur of tigers from the jungles he disdains—
who sees only that which he wishes to see,
so consummate, so filled with majesty, is he.

If this robe were made, I would tire of wearing it.

Unmade, I wear it still,
and it is glorious.
In this robe I stride across my foot soldiers' backs.
I allow my lieutenants to lift me to the ramparts.
I show myself to my people.
They are aghast. They are inflamed.
They swoon.
As I raise my granite arms and set the yellow dragon soaring,
they understand who I am.

They understand.
I am.
The world is one.

939

It's April 1944,
and Mary Ellen Nutt Beal is conducting a ladies' luncheon
    in her home on Ridge Avenue in Evanston, Illinois.
When you peek past the portières in the dining room,
all that you can see around the table
    is pink (flesh) and gray (curls) and navy (outfits),
this navy—
just right for the crisp clean look of spring.

Seated at the head of the table,
a mahogany behemoth purchased from the Ursuline nuns
    in the French Quarter before her husband Wood
    moved her north,
Mary Ellen wears a navy silk dress patterned in
    yellow and white daisies.
The outfit is not exactly what the February Vogue has meant,
featuring Gene Tierney in a crisp clean navy suit,
with a crisp clean ascot in navy and white stripes,
and a crisp clean cloche in matching stripes,
tied off at the side with a big dramatic bow.

No. At Mary Ellen's luncheon, where the ladies are the age of
    Gene Tierney's mother, or more,
the look is not so much crisp and clean as it is coddled
    and stuffed,
but the ladies are wearing navy as Vogue has said they should.

Adele Wilkinson's suit in lightweight navy wool
    boasts a three-quarter jacket and an amethyst brooch,
while poor dear Mabel Eddy has put new buttons
    on her old blue crêpe.
Mary Fall and Mary Brown Fall are not the same lady,
but they're wearing the same navy,
and so is Anne Scott, who's nodding off again.

Edith Rogers is chasing aspic round her salad plate,
and everyone is trying not to listen to Madge, Madge Campbell,
whose romantic exploits at her age are certainly
        not seemly, and probably not possible,
and as for Madge's hat, it's a horror.
It looks like a lily pond, or a bayou, or a bog,
on top of whose blue and pink and taupe satin swatches,
the hatter has affixed a green satin frog.

Mary Ellen knows what is what.
She knows you do not say to one of your oldest friends, and
        most persistent annoyances,
from whose first husband Towne, shortly before their divorce,
        Wood bought this house in 1910,
Mary Ellen knows you do not say, Madge, go home.
(In many ways, Madge thinks she *is* at home,
        although the house is firmly Mary Ellen's and will always be.)
Mary Ellen knows you do not say, Madge, that hat
        is ruining my luncheon.
She knows you do not say, Madge, I am going to scream
        if you do not take that hat off right now.

No, you sit there and suffer,
reminding yourself that the royal family has not quit London
        for the bombs,
that your father kept the plantation going after the War
        Between the States,
that you got this house back, on your own, a second time,
        fourteen years after Wood's partners made you sell it at his death.

All to entertain a frog.

Well, only the hostess goes hatless at luncheons,
so the horror will have to stay on Madge's head.
Mary Ellen is asserting her right of ownership, her authority,
in allowing Madge to continue to wear that thing.
This is victory for Mary Ellen, total triumph,
her own gracious blitzkrieg,
but only Adele will ever know, when they talk the luncheon over
    tomorrow morning on the phone.

Ah, what are friends for but to drive you mad,
and make you feel better,
and just keep you going no matter what?—
and now here is Agda with that lovely lemon angel-food,
and Mary Ellen will sit facing away from Madge, at quite another table,
    when the ladies play bridge after luncheon,
and maybe, just maybe (she will have to think about this),
Mary Ellen will invite her grandson, visiting from Pittsburgh,
    to dig up a worm in the garden for Auntie Madge's frog.

Hah!
Even if she doesn't,
(and she knows she won't; no proper Southern lady ever would),
the thought of the worm,
along with Agda's lovely lemon angel-food,
quite restores Mary Ellen's sense of hospitality.

972

Last night I stitched a corner of a room with 3722,
a deep apricot taupe,
and with 3328, a shade that is brighter and peachier,
and now, tonight, for a stairwell bordering this juicy room,
I put in 972.

Do you know 972?

This chrome is a yellow you could walk to China on,
a bounty for which you could stamp your foot
    right through the floor
when the princess, who's been spinning strands of 972, inquires,
"You like this color, Rumpelstiltskin?"

I like this color, Princess.

For this majestic gold I will keep my temper.
Stay here. Say you win.
Be your servant, be your slave,
just to keep in touch with all this egg-yolk yellow,
just to keep my hands on
all this glory stuff.

991

Every red haired woman in the world has worn this green.

When the movies went to Ireland in 1952,
a chorus line of lady leprechauns tricked out in 991—
satin caps and satin shorts and snappy satin vests—
greeted Gene Kelly as he danced off the ship,
and down the pier,
and through the town,
and over the hill,
slick two-leaf clovers of green rumps blossoming behind.

Blue-green, really, an August color in the shade,
deep shade, a shade of the texture and the longing and the
       long afternoons in the Alabama of Kurt Weill.
There is smoke in this green, smoke and romance,
       as Susan Hayward in a hoop skirt strolls the verandah
       impatient for her swain.

So what we've got here is a movie green,
the designer Edith Head swirling out a bolt of 991—
always in satin, only in satin—
and draping it around Rita Hayworth,
who is perfect, and smooth, like a woman made of peaches,
peaches and cognac and vanilla ice cream.

How can God make such beauty?

How can God resist?

The Whole Class

When I consider the colors I have written poems for,
I see a photo of a class of children in 1948.
You can tell the leaders—those who are big,
or well dressed, or not intimidated by the camera:
the girl with the ribbon in her long blonde hair,
the tall boy with the rakish smile,
the pretty twins.

If these children were the colors I have written poems for,
I would say I know them well;
I would say they do good work.
Yes, I would say, I regard them as my stars.

But I would also say I love the rest of the class,
those whose features and abilities are not developed yet,
the kids who tend to look like each other
until you get to know them,
until you hold their hands
and take them for a walk.

So, if you should ask me, "Which colors do you love?,"
I would have to say, "All."
I would have to say, "Here are all my friends,"
as I take from the drawers of Grandmother's Italian chest
the bags and boxes in which I keep my floss,
then overturn them on the rug
where the colors jumble together in the sun,
humming with contentment—
like jewels unearthed from Ali Baba's cave,
like kids set free from school.